Every
Best
Day

My life Adventure as
a Teenager with
Bi-Polar Disorder

-David DiBelardino

Deciding to elevate every day possibilities for good, instead of dreading another impending meltdown

Every day has challenges as well as triumphs, finding the keys to lift up a bad day is a treasure.

Hi my name is David. I have Bi-Polar Mood Disorder. I also have Schizoaffective Disorder.

I want to show what is in the mind of a person who has this set of thoughts.

I am blessed not to be shut away, but given opportunities in a safe space. Knowing my limits has helped me.

I have discovered a great set of tricks and tips that help calm emotions that can surge out of control for no rational reason.

Some days are GREAT one moment, then AWFUL the next moment—for no discernable reason.

Knowing when to leave a situation is critical. I have permission to LEAVE any situation when I feel a surge of BIG, SCARY emotions come on.

Have a plan in place before church starts (wait by the car), have a plan in place before going into a theme park (code word RED), have a plan in place before going into Target (code word RED).

PLANNING AHEAD
WILL ALWAYS BE
GOOD.

I work with my mom to
make sure we can get our
errands done. But this
means planning!

My mom knows I will
not overuse the CODE
WORDS, and I know she
will leave the second I
say them. This makes me
feel safe and loved.

Bi-Polar kids think in terms of SUPERALTIVES. We do not have any average emotions, days, or reactions.

Every event is THE BEST or THE WORST!

Every meal is THE YUMMIEST or the GROSSEST!

Every person is a FRIEND or an ENEMY!

Accepting the fact that waves of intense emotions will swamp the best of days is helpful.

Knowing that a better day could be right around the corner helps also.

Learning to control my response to daily events is what this book is all about.

When your Mood is Out of Bounds

actions to take that help

Helpful Actions

getting outside

walking

eating (outside)

breathing in my nose
and out my mouth

the right music

talking with a
trusted person

sunset time

anything in nature

quiet time in my room

When your mood is Out
of Bounds

These will HURT:

People who yell

People who lecture

Staying where the event
occurred

Hiding in a closet

Breaking and destroying
things

If you are upset

How to calm down

Talk with a trusted person

Avoid an angry person who lectures

Play or read or get involved in a hobby

Go for a walk outside

Exercise outside

Watch TV/movies that are calming, funny or interesting-like PBS Kids

Drinking hot chocolate or hot tea

Making cookies + eating cookies

Chew gum

How to calm down some one else

Look them in the eye

Gently touch them

Listen without interrupting

Listen without judgment

Offer a glass of water

Take them outside, away
from the original setting

Speak softly- speak slowly

Speak from a position of love

A present always helps- even if it is a note

Know you can validate someone as a loved/ valuable person and not agree with their emotional reaction to an event!

Ideas for hobbies you
may become passionate
about: suggestions

-board games

-Legos

-reading

-strategy video games

-collecting comics,
stamps, coins, records

Good habits

- drink water
  stay hydrated

- walk every day

- notice nature

Develop a daily
ROUTINE

A ROUTINE is a set of tasks you can depend on to happen. This gives stability to your day. A ROUTINE can be flexible, can be changed, and can be modified.

My daily ROUTINE:

Sleep in!

Drink coffee

Eat

School work

Walk

Eat

Free time

My ROUTINE can change when we go on vacation, have guests, or if I have an appointment. But I like knowing what is going to be 'next' every day.

Getting a job will help you feel useful, have purpose.

Not all jobs come with a paycheck.

A job can be for a neighbor, church family, or friend.

Picking up pinecones and sticks after a storm is a job.

Walking a dog is a job.

Vacuuming the living room is a job.

Mowing the lawn is an awful job.

If you get paid, GREAT!

But even if you do not receive any money, a job is still an important thing to have.

If you have mental disorder of any kind it is important to have trusted people.

A trusted person will not judge you for yucky thoughts.

You do not have to have more than one trusted person, even one trusted person is a treasure.

Made in the USA
Columbia, SC
07 June 2018